Stealing Wonder

A Rhyming Race
to
Capture Grace

By

Linda Ann Nickerson

Stealing Wonder

A Rhyming Race to Capture Grace

Gait
House
Press

Published in the United States by Gait House Press.

Printed in the United States of America.

2013

ISBN: 0615939686

ISBN-13: 978-0615939681

Cover Illustration:
Vintage sketch – public domain

Dedication

This collection of verses is dedicated with much love to those treasured individuals who have laid a legacy of faith in my life.

Author's Preface

I'm not a perfect Christian. Sometimes, I'm
not even a very good Christian at all. But
God loves me enough to hold onto me,
even in those times.

Sometimes I feel as if I am stealing wonder,
because I live with the undeserved grace
offered by a God who is abundant love
personified. No matter what happens in
this mortal season, I am already blessed
with immeasurably more than I deserve,
simply because He calls me His child and
invites me to share forever with Him.

What a promise.

I have been blind, and now I see. I have

been weak, and He has made me strong. I have been crushed, and He has cherished me. I have been broken, and He has made me joyful. I have been rejected, and He has restored me. I have been lost, and He has found me.

And He is not finished with me yet.

If you're reading these words, then He's not finished with you, either. He's just getting warmed up, and it's gonna be great.

Watch and see what He has in store for you.

The Scriptures overflow with blessed accounts of God rebuilding human lives for Heaven's glory.

Here's one of my favorites:

Being confident of this very thing, that he which hath begun a good work in you will perform it until the day of Jesus Christ. (Philippians 1:6, KJV)

Thank God.

What a relief it is to know that He is still doing this wonderful work in us and that He promises not to quit.

I am so not worthy. But that is pretty much the point, isn't it?

Will it shock you, if I suggest that maybe unbelievers are onto something, when they complain that Christians are hypocrites? Perhaps we are – at least, if we claim to be

Christ-like.

If we were already holy, as He is holy, then we would not need redemption. We could go without grace.

Only we can't.

Even the most saintly believers slip up. In fact, those humble ones would likely be the first to admit it.

That's the heart of God's good news. Isn't that why the Lord gave His own life on a dreaded cross to buy us back from ourselves? Would He pay such a dear cost, if it wasn't necessary?

Hallelujah. What a Savior.

This collection of verses reveals part of my

personal journey. Lines detail ups and downs, victories and struggles, desires to be faithful and times of faithlessness. In each instance, the Beloved One has been there, taking my hand and my heart and drawing me back.

Pretending is futile.

If there is one lesson the Father of mercy impresses most often on my heart, it is this: The longer I know Him, the more I see how unlike Him I still am. But He continues to call me closer, especially when I have wandered far from Him.

He reaches out and welcomes those who know we need Him.

I hope and pray these words will encourage you in your own path of faith.

All I know is this: He came.

My Redeemer called my name –

Took my claim to blame and shame,

And I will never be the same.

I am stealing wonder.

I'm grabbing onto blessings I did not earn. And I am clinging fast to a treasure that will last for all eternity, offered by the only One who merits such reward.

Maybe you are stealing wonder too. It's there for the taking, given by the only One who keeps His promises – forever and Amen.

Linda Ann Nickerson

Contents

Stealing Wonder

A Rhyming Race
to
Capture Grace

1

Amazing Rephrasing

Most confidantes deserve not trust;

Self-centered friendship is unjust.

But one Companion merits more,

The One who knocks on my heart's door.

I need not speak in "Thou's" and "Thee's."

I simply cry out, "Father, please!"

He knows the longings of my soul —

To rest in Him and be made whole.

I fumble with my simple thought,

Afraid my dreams may come to naught,

Until He hears mere words of mine

And translates to a tongue divine.

The Holy Spirit intercedes

Before the throne to lay my needs.

Unhindered by false human flair,

He crafts a Heaven-worthy prayer.

Although my phrasings may fall short,

Angelic forces make no sport.

They join all praises to the King

And make the realms of Heaven ring.

And God the Father, above all,

He stoops to listen to my call.

So tickled that I love Him back,

The Lord supplies all that I lack.

2

A Carpenter's Song

The Carpenter builds from His heart

To transform my rubble to art.

Each pass of His plane

Does follow the grain,

His beauty and grace to impart.

No hammer of harm does He wield,

Although to the same did He yield.

Instead, He constructs,

Rebuilds and instructs,

Till His new creation's revealed.

The process may take all my days,

As I pull against all His stays.

With masterful hands,

He saws, and He sands,

Creating a portrait of praise.

3

The Chimera's Calling

I've never aimed at fitting in,
As instantly I knew.
My doodles darted from my pen,
As inspiration grew.

Still, joy surprises past all rights,
Incongruous, it grows.
Beyond the city lights and sights,
It sheds its gladsome glows.

As a chimera, hybrid born,
'Twixt feral, fine and fair,
I will not utter words of scorn
For Him who meets me there.

Though fiercest frenzies shout my name,

Inviting me to ire,

An inner calling draws its claim

And calls me ever higher.

4

Crossroads

I love to speed, get it in gear,

So why are we still standing here?

My engine's roaring; hear it keen.

God, won't You send a light that's green?

I have great plans, Lord. Can't You see?

You want to come along with me?

Why must I rest and wait so long

To find Your will, when I'm headstrong?

So shall I signal to the right?

I'm holding on with all my might.

I'd love to stomp upon the gas.

My time is slipping through the glass.

All right, I'll stop and wait for You.

Despite my plans, I have no clue.

Here at the crossroads, in midstream,

Things aren't always what they seem.

You lead me in a slower pace,

By silent waters, secret space.

My motor roars and longs for more,

But greater things have You in store.

5

Day Trip

The greatest solace I have found,

With sacred secrets, strongly bound,

Cannot be found in tattered talk –

But in a simple country walk.

Appearances mislead and feign.

The finest offerings oft are plain.

As seasons whirl our course along,

False tigers tempts us to the wrong.

The peril of unspoken dream

May taunt and tease with empty gleam.

Apparent defect draws a sneer,

As youngsters play, cajole and jeer.

A laundry list of lingered doubt

Does trim my trellis round-about,

Supplanting blossoms from their hold

Unless I banish it full bold.

A moment's recreation may

Prevent such lies from holding sway.

Regained perspective, now and then,

May cause my soul to smile again.

My Company, He calls me forth.

To reassure, He gives me worth.

My own society of two

Does energize, transform, renew.

We stroll the meadows, trails and wood,

Regarding nether's neighborhood.

He points my paces all aright,

So long as He is in my sight.

The rest may follow or may fold

Beneath examples yet untold.

Myself, though scorned, I'll stake my

ground

Upon that Rock that bids me bound.

6

Dream of Flying

To dream of flying over all,
To enter the next phase.
To rise and fall, a free-for-all,
To step out of the race.

The trumpet calls. The angel sings.
I ride astride a horse with wings.
Go face to face with King of Kings,
Who takes His place o'er everything.

To dream of flying over all,
To enter the next phase.
To rise and fall, a free-for-all,
To step out of the race.

Then trials fall away like dust.

My great achievements prove a bust.

I look upon them with disgust

And value just the One I trust.

To dream of flying over all,

To enter the next phase.

To rise and fall, a free-for-all,

To step out of the race.

7

Editorial License

My days are slipping faster, and
The glass is running out of sand.
What will you write about me when
My lips have prayed their last "Amen"?

Obituaries leave much out;
They leave a lot of room for doubt –
A few short lines to spell a span,
A life reduced, flash in the pan.

Credentials listed on a page
And kinfolk listed, name and age.
A few statistics cited there
To show achievements, if you care.

I hope my life will mean much more
Than these bare facts will underscore.
I want to leave a mark behind,
A legacy for folks to find.

My hope is that you won't see me,
But Him who lives inside, home free.
My His forgiveness hold your heart,
If we should fail before we part.

Will you forget me when I've left,
Or will you be bereaved, bereft?
Remember only all the good
And not when we've misunderstood.

May grace erase the untold ills
And many battles of our wills.
I pray His peace will seal your soul
Until in Him you are made whole.

8

The End of Fear

Scaly-skinned devils that rage in the night,
Spewing their fires with endless delight,
Consuming their enemies, both left and
right –
These are the creatures that caused me
such fright.

A long, jagged tail tossed itself in my way.
I wrestled and fought it, to keep it at bay.
It slithered and reared up to blow me
away,
So I fell to my knees, and I started to pray.

Father, forgive me, for I have done wrong.

My feet, they have gone where they did
not belong.
My mind and my heart have neglected
Your song.
Please help me, for I know not how to be
strong.

A great gentle hand lifted me from the dirt.
With sweet loving-kindness, He raised me,
unhurt,
And brushed smoky ashes away from my
shirt.
He said, "Look to Me, and be ever alert!"

For the dragon may prowl and may seek to
devour.
He may even think he has magical power.
But his time is coming, the day he will
cower.
As evil will vanish, the whole earth will
flower.

The King will return, and the heads He will
sever
Of all who would fight Him or even
endeavor.
No others can touch Him again; they may
never.
His Kingdom will reign then – forever and
ever.

9

Facing the Dragons

We hope to make a splendid splash,
To rake in blessings, boon and cash,
Till dragon bids us into clash,
Releasing violent backlash.

We recognize the need to fight,
To stand our ground or flee in flight.
Still, do we dare the dark with light
Or banish truth and melt to night?

For ageless and contagious be
The talons sharp of strife's degree.
We may be caught in his debris,
If we deign not to disagree.

What dragon fight we, if we can?

Will he be monster, demon, man?

Where might we find a battle plan

For conflict since the world began?

When bitterness may yet take root,

Devouring us in disrepute,

Infecting us with violent fruit?

Will we seek solace absolute?

What worthy Ally bids us cease,

Inviting us to strife's release?

May we diminish, He increase,

For only then may we find peace.

10

The Finest Wine

I'm tempted not much to imbibe,

Although it's not a diatribe.

The fire water makes me reel,

And I don't like the way I feel.

For motion sickness, standing still,

Is guaranteed, if I should swill.

A pounding head will follow next,

A necessary aftertext.

And yet, sometimes the fruit of vine

Can be delightful, as we dine.

A little sip of something light

Accompanies a tasty bite.

The sweetest wine of all the years

Was mingled with the Savior's tears,

He poured it out in love to save,

Before He overcame the grave.

Now He awaits the great command,

A chalice in His nail-scarred hand.

His bride prepares to meet her love,

When trumpet calls from up above.

No palate ever tasted such,

As granted by the Master's touch.

He'll offer vintage without cease,

And we will toast the Prince of Peace.

11

Fresh

I once was innocent and clean
Before I learned my way –
Before I yearned for things between,
And then I turned away.

Because I died, you may be whole.
I rose, so you can rise.
When angels call and clouds unfold,
Come. Meet me in the skies.

My feet, they lead me far afield,
My hands, they reach for more.
My eyes, they seek beyond Your shield
To things I should abhor.

I dream of days when I'll desire

Your honor and Your face –

To bow and lift You higher and higher,

Your Name no more disgrace.

Because I died, you may be whole.

I rose, so you can rise.

When angels call and clouds unfold,

Come. Meet me in the skies.

Give me a glimpse of purity,

Of glory from above,

That I may rest in surety,

Your confidence and love.

For I believe, but help my doubt,

Oh, take my failings. Cast them out.

My heart knows not what it's about.

Give me desire to be devout.

Because I died, you may be whole.

I rose, so you can rise.

When angels call and clouds unfold,

Come. Meet me in the skies.

12

A Glimmer of Grace

He welcomes me to an empty chair,
As wings unseen glide with us there.
My drought is drenched with simple
prayer.
A glimmer is greater than gold.

Fierce fury flies, and guilt departs,
Along with the accuser's darts.
I'm rescued by the Prince of hearts.
A glimmer is greater than gold.

The angels whisper, "Free at last."
My winter's tale has lost its blast.
For love divine is unsurpassed.

A glimmer is greater than gold.

His mercy leaves no room for doubt.

My darkest memories, now cast out.

Lord, make me evermore devout.

A glimmer is greater than gold.

With thankful heart, no longer torn,

I rise to meet the purest morn.

Clothed in His light, may truth adorn.

A glimmer is greater than gold.

13

Grime and Grace

I've stumbled into things unseen.
No steaming bath can make me clean.
My fine appearance, a smokescreen,
Pretending Heavenly hygiene.

For each Commandment, I have spurned,
Resolving good and then returned.
Where righteousness may be concerned,
I cannot say I've lived and learned.

I

Loving God above the rest?
That has been a daily test.

II

Idol worship , claiming stuff?

I never seem to have enough.

III

Using God's great Name in vain?

Perhaps I said a word profane.

IV

Keeping Sunday in my heart?

My calendar is torn apart.

V

Treating parents with respect?

How often do I disconnect?

VI

Murder, rage, or hate someone?

What happens when I jump the gun?

VII

0

0

0

Adultery I have not tried,
But have I been dissatisfied?

VIII
Stealing comes in many styles.
Will I go the extra miles?

IX
Testifying, telling lies?
Have I tried to rationalize?

X
Desiring someone else's things?
Am I entangled in such strings?

Perhaps I'm guilty on all counts,
By many pounds or just an ounce.
The Judge could justly me renounce
And "Ever Guilty" me pronounce.

I've stumbled into things obscene.

No steaming bath can make me clean.

And yet, He died to intervene,

To offer Heavenly hygiene.

So, purified, I freely stand.

My Savior takes me by the hand

And leads me to another land

With grace I dare not understand.

14

A Head of Truth

As cabbage leaves, curled 'gainst the night,

Our blessings may seem locked up tight.

They may look lush,

But out of touch,

Until we set our sights aright.

For, thinking we may toe the line,

We stage a scene of wrong design.

Indulgence pleas

For lives of ease

With lucky leaves and carefree time.

A Gardener tenders every frill,

But first, the soil He must till.

May joys be found

In welcome ground

That readies to accept His will.

What flowered kale may us instruct,

If we our doubtings may deduct –

To persevere

And flourish here

Before the cabbage has been plucked?

15

Heart of the Gardener

The Gardener's heart is evergreen,
And yet, His hands are ne'er unclean.
He tends the ground. He sends the rain
And softens soil to grow His grain.

The Sower plants His seeds in love
And urges them with rays above.
Then, as they germinate and grow,
He nourishes from roots below.

As seedlings sprout and spread their wings,
The Gardener positively sings.
His heart is blessed to watch them bloom,
Emerging from the garden's womb.

Oh, how the Gardener's heart is torn

To see Creation lost in scorn,

His blossoms spent by bourgeoisie

And plantings littered by debris.

But we continue, unawares,

Refocused on our own affairs.

How can we take for granted such,

When tended by the Gardener's touch?

16

High Horse of Heaven

He rides upon a spotless mount.

His name is ever True.

The Faithful One, most paramount,

Returns for me and you.

With nail-scarred hands, He holds the rein.

His wounded feet hold fast.

Although He conquered death and pain,

The scars will ever last.

Above the clouds, He pirouettes.

A trumpet sounds the call.

The King whose blood redeemed our debts

Has triumphed over all.

In glowing robes and starry crown,

He gallops His joyride.

The time has come; He canters down

To beckon for His bride.

Then, seated on high Heaven's horse,

The Bridegroom and His love,

They share a ride on glory's course

To regions far above.

17

Holier Than Now

Why do I ever box You in,

As if to shirk Your discipline,

Although Your oil of healing balm

Might mend, restore and ever calm?

Conflicted in my deepest soul,

I long to let You have control –

To rise above all that I fear,

Press ever closer and revere.

Instead, I swap ideas with fools,

Who resurrect all rotten rules.

Perhaps they think me stupid still

And hope to sway me from Your will.

In conversations, just we two,

I fall in love again with You.

Lord, make me evermore desire

To be made holy by Your fire.

18

How Long?

"Come and sit with Me awhile,"
My Beloved said.
"I have missed your sweetest smile.
It seems that it has fled."

He'd waited in our private spot.
I hadn't even seen.
How long had He been there? I thought,
And where else have I been?

His longing brought me to my knees,
And I began to pray.
"Forgive me, Lord, I've missed you.
Please!"

My sorrows flew away.

There, in His company, I knew
His love dashed my despair.
Our time together, overdue,
Brought joy beyond compare.

How had I passed Him by before,
Not noticing His plea,
When fellowship and love secure
Had waited there for me?

19

Hungry Sheep

Some Sunday sermons make us laugh.

They raise a cheery mood.

And still you show the narrow path

When you serve solid food.

Though babes the mildest milk desire,

With feedings every hour,

The more mature reach ever higher,

Craving higher power.

So bring it on, and throw it down

With vegetables and meat.

Those in the pew may fret and frown;

They just need more to eat.

Our ears are tickled, to be sure,

With humor and with fun.

But real nutrition will endure

When we our course have run.

The Lord, He knows this fine cuisine

Is harder to prepare.

But minerals and real protein

Will fuel a powered prayer.

20

In My Father's Field

Father, find me in Your field,

Where Your mercies are revealed.

There Your secrets have been sealed

And all hurtings may be healed.

Take my hand, and lead me there

In the gently stirring air.

Place Your peace on my despair.

I will follow anywhere.

How I long to do much more,

Any plans You have in store –

Dauntless, driven to the core,

Serving You forevermore.

Touch my eyes, and let me see

Visions of Your love for me.

Speak Your truth, and I'll agree,

As You carry me home free.

Plant my feet here on Your sod,

In Your Presence, duly awed.

Place me in Your promenade,

Glorifying only God.

21

Integrity Identified

My oldest friend, she will not fudge,

Not disconnect, pretend, misjudge.

Duplicity, it has no place –

Her highest plea, to live by grace.

Securely plugged into the Source,

She waits. The Master charts the course.

As Jesus holds the power cords,

This woman's work He fuels, rewards.

Though storms of stress, in crowded rage,

May clatter, crash, to disengage,

No breach of confidence or myth,

No necessary ill forthwith

May daunt this darer from her goal.

For she is sure He holds her soul.

His Word is tucked inside her heart

With wondered wisdom to impart.

22

Interceding Beats Misreading

My friends, they open up my eyes

With earnest prayers and groaning sighs.

For even when I cannot pray,

These faithful lampholders ne'er stray.

Beseeching from the Source of Light,

I wrestled with Him through the night.

A foggy fortnight passed me by

With cirrus shadowing one eye.

A sudden shade eclipsed my days,

Attempting to confuse my ways.

I'd blink and stare and stop to see,

But vision still eluded me.

As fear's own forces raised their swords,

With daggers forged from daunting words,

I sketched a line and stood my ground,

My own lost lens to be refound.

Then, tracing images by heart,

I drew upon a missing part.

For other hands, they held me dear

By interceding through to clear.

True vision rests in mind control,

Perceiving insights of the soul.

Mere repetition, prayer is not,

Nor unexpected faith begot.

Pure promises may still await

For miracles, not yet too late.

No monster may exhaust the beam,

For sights may not be all they seem.

Though days and weeks may be a blur,

My faith is focused. I concur.

The Healer's power will persist.

Lampholders: Thanks for the assist.

23

Lead Me to the Rock

Rock of refuge, hear my call.

Hold my hand that I not fall.

Guard my heart, and make it Thine.

Lead me in the path divine.

Earth and Heaven, You display.

Work Your wonders here today.

Boldly, as I face the beast,

Do I ask for Your release.

Set my feet upon Your rock.

Guide my footsteps and my talk.

Keep deceit and lying oath

From my lips' indulgent growth.

As offenders sharpen swords,

With their most malicious words,

May Your Rock their blades scrape dull,

That their phrasings be made null.

You my firmest foothold be,

Evermore, eternally.

Rock Almighty, ever strong,

Be Thou honored by my song.

24

The Lighthouse

The beacon warns the ships at sea
Of dangers on the coast.
A lighthouse, that's what I would be
To influence and host.

The world is dark, with hazards great
And unseen perils too.
Give me a beam to flash through hate
And make my peace with You.

Just set my lamp upon the mount
To shine on every wave.
And make my four-score annums count,
Another life to save.

But if my lamp grows cracked and cold,

No glory to reflect,

Then draw me back, You to behold,

And me to genuflect.

I have no light to guide a boat

Or even just for me.

But you may keep us all afloat

And lead us 'cross the sea.

25

Mended and Commended

Plunging wound, I needed healing,

Gangrene growing, blood congealing.

Flesh escaping in a haze,

I recounted all my days.

Laden with a load, I sorrowed –

Ill-contentment, bought and borrowed.

Inner scorn, my truest friend,

Trying hard, truth to suspend.

Then a flash flew through my soul.

Truth and grace were my parole.

Who could love me fully such,

Heal me wholly with His touch?

'Twas the Master Healer, He,

Who designed eternity.

Looking deep into my dark,

With His holy healing spark.

All I know is this: He came.

My Redeemer called my name –

Took my claim to blame and shame,

And I will never be the same.

26

My Stand

For decades, he has tried to bust

The joy inside my soul

With accusations, broken trust,

And eyes as black as coal.

With dark designs and deepest doubts,

This evil plotting ploy

Was aiming for a falling out –

To kill, steal and destroy.

And his intentions sinister

Did cause my soul to tire,

But truth makes me a minister

And calls me ever higher.

The One within is stronger still;

'Tis He who keeps me whole.

There's none can sway or slay my will

When He is in control.

So get behind me. Be forewarned,

If I may be so bold.

Although you've spit and scoffed and

scorned,

I seek a greater goal.

With shield in hand, I take my stand.

The night begins to shake.

With just one Word, the Name is heard.

May there be no mistake.

The sneering one, he turns to run.

He cannot take me now.

For he has wholly come undone.

All I can say is, "Wow."

Perhaps he plans his next onslaught.

I hope to be prepared.

With victory begun, blood-bought,

I need not be ensnared.

27

No Mistake

A flimsy, fleeting spark of fright,

A cluttered cloud of broken sight,

Forbidden climate's candlelight,

Can scatter truth and doubt incite.

The raging monster bares his claws.

He rises up and stomps his paws.

The mystery, it looms because

The mad beast stands against all laws.

To pilot truth upon its trail,

To foster faith, our Holy Grail,

Emitting diamonds past the pale,

No simple sunny lines prevail.

A mere misnomer shakes the ground,

As rumors swirl the world around.

The faithful one is honor-bound

To wait and watch the Lord astound.

A cup of wonder cannot cure,

Despite the finest connoisseur,

Who proves to be an amateur.

When danger dares, he's yet unsure.

The image blurs. We cannot tell:

Is this a promise or farewell?

The monster roars, ills to propel,

But hope is whispering, "Do tell."

Make no mistake. We make a choice.

Ignore the rumble, loudest voice.

Don't be deterred by dark decoys.

Your miracle awaits. Rejoice.

28

Not Shaken, But Stirred

A question plagued me since my youth –
How worthless chaff established root
To stand and grow and bear its fruit,
Contagious evil absolute.

Yet beauty planted by Your hand,
Obeying fully Your command,
May struggle, as if in quicksand,
Still reaching skyward for homeland.

So evil prospers, even here,
As weeds advance, inciting fear.
They choke out life and bend the ear.
At what point will they disappear?

As blossoms fail, we stretch and age,

Refusing to engage ill's rage.

Our roots hold fast against rampage,

Forever planted in truth's page.

The world considers us absurd,

The weirdest ones that may be heard.

But we cling closely to Your Word

To be unshaken, only stirred.

29

On the Road

I'm living, longing. Take me back.

My heart, it must rewind, backtrack.

In vaguest reveries, I find

Your tender care most underlined.

The greatest day I've ever known

Was when I claimed You as my own.

I vowed to serve You, then forgot.

Though You've been faithful, I have not.

The blacktop ribbon, hard and fast,

Draws me to danger at full blast.

Its dotted markings lull my soul,

As I slip into cruise control.

What happened to the glory days?
They've disappeared in smoky haze.
Once fearless, clutching to Your hand,
I'd follow You to no-man's land.

Since then, my heart has taken flight,
Caressing clouds in oversight.
The road below, the sky above,
They lured me from my own first love.

Although my hands have gripped the
wheel,
I find it harder to conceal:
The obstacles within my lane
Are sent to make the pathway plain.

I'm living, longing. Take me back.
My heart, it must rewind, backtrack.
Remove the shade that blocks my view.
I only live to follow You.

30

A Poet's Plea

Great God, Creator absolute,

I beg You, make me resolute.

Just write Your Word upon my heart,

That I may never stray, depart.

You ask no other sacrifice,

No payment or admission price.

For You've redeemed me, made me whole,

And marked my name upon Your scroll.

Equip my feet that I may stand,

Proclaiming truth in any land.

Lord, clear my ear that I may hear

Your words of comfort, ever dear.

Unseal my lips that I may shout

Your righteousness. Make me devout.

Restore my calling and my quill.

Conform them both to suit Your will.

Your blessings yet exceed each sum,

So humbly to Your heart I come.

If You should never bless again,

Redemption is enough. Amen.

31

Prescription Post-Its

In serendipity profane,

We swim in sinful shadows' stain –

Go with the flow,

Although we know

It swings us closer to the drain.

It seems an inconvenient truth

That we pretend extended youth.

We sneer at fate

And fabricate

Sweet insincerities uncouth.

For purposes medicinal,

We daily dose till we're unwell.

The tightest knot

May be forgot,

If we just label it most swell.

A leaf with stellar points aligned

Grants temporary peace of mind.

Discoveries

Of broken ease

Will soon return, lest we be blind.

So, satisfied, as lazy lambs,

We're prey to predatory scams.

We gobble lies

With no surprise.

We're unprepared for life's exams.

If I could live in era past,

I'd choose to let tradition last.

World-weary now,

Will we allow

Our freedoms torn away so fast?

A sweet solution is festooned,

Although our morals we've marooned.

Let's tape the gash

With festive flash

And hope to hide a fatal wound.

32

Pure or Painted?

I wish my heart were ever pure,
My mind and thoughts untainted,
Except this world and its allure
My attitude have painted.

My focus shifts from right to wrong
And often in-between.
I'd rather carry Heaven's song
And worship the Unseen.

This mortal frame, it drags me down,
Though destiny is sure.
I'll leave this desolate ghost town.
Till then, Lord, keep me pure.

33

Redeemed from Religion

I've been redeemed, in Jesus' Name,
From every false religion's game.
For Jesus took my sin and shame,
And I will never be the same.

I once was bound by Bible thumpers,
Wearing large, white-collared jumpers.
These I stitched all by myself,
From fabrics purchased off the shelf.

For years, I memorized each rule,
From grandest scale to miniscule.
I'd scorn the mirror when I fell,
Pronouncing myself ne'er-do-well.

I'd glance askance at holy folk
And think it was the meanest joke.
I knew I'd never make the grade,
And so I build a barricade.

Exhausted, I would try to stand
And measure up to each command.
But daily, I would face a fault
That brought my progress to a halt.

Now I am loosed from legal ties
That worry, stress, and paralyze.
Once captive, I have been set free
To follow Him who pardoned me.

And here's the big surprise of all:
This liberty comes with a call.
The Lord has lifted by law load
And I desire to live His code.

I will not follow our of fear,

But still, I long to persevere.

Obedience can be renewed

By simple love and gratitude.

I've been redeemed, in Jesus' Name,

From every false religion's game.

For Jesus took my sin and shame,

And I will never be the same.

34

Soul-Worn

My soul grew old before its prime,

Bespattered, stained, and gored with

grime,

From anguished dreams and darkest crime,

My soul, the refugee.

The calendar aged slower still,

My heart entwined with vines until

The tangling tendrils choked my will,

My soul in lock and key.

Those nearest couldn't comprehend

My soul, descended to its end.

Instead, they tried to recommend,

My soul to oversee.

A silent voice, as if on cue,

A gentle saber pierced me through,

Unchained my pain and made me new.

My soul, at least, was free.

35

Tuning In

For years, I was both deaf and mute,
In unawareness absolute.
I strove to live the best I could,
Unconscious and misunderstood.

The calendar consumed my mind.
I looked for life, but did not find.
Success, elusive, held my heart,
Awaiting still a missing part.

Obeying rules and discipline,
Content that such would earn my in,
I still ignored a higher call,
With spirit launching overhaul.

Until a sound disturbed my sleep,
"As ye doth sow, so shall ye reap."
Disheartened that He'd call my bluff,
I simply couldn't do enough.

But grace enveloped all my need,
As He began to intercede.
I saw my strivings turn to ash,
A giant bulk of balderdash.

And from the embers, sprung a root
That soon began to bear much fruit.
My life, it gained a fresh aroma,
Wakened from a soul-deep coma.

36

Upper Room Unbooked

My daybook is full. Get in line.

No time for the bread or the wine.

Frustrations ensnare

Till I climb the stair

To privately offer my shrine.

No temple of gold does He ask.

I need not perform holy task.

Just stop – step apart –

And open my heart,

Removing my own feigning mask.

What intimacy may await?

How deeply may God then relate,

If schedules would pause

And hopes for applause?

Oh, may I arrive not too late.

About the Author

An award-winning poet and prolific writer, holding a B.A. in English and an M.S. in Journalism, Linda Ann has worked as a professional writer for more than three decades. She has also taught creative writing classes.

Linda Ann Nickerson writes news and feature columns for several well-known websites. Her published portfolio includes well over 5,000 web articles, as well as countless print pieces.

Blogs owned by Linda Ann Nickerson include:

Delightfully Amiss: Berzerkians Gone Amok and Finding the Funk in Dysfunction

Heart of a Ready Writer

Nickers and Ink

Practically at Home

The Mane Point

Working in Words

and more.

Other titles by this author

- *25 Top Tips for Promoting Your Equestrian Event: Get the Herd Out*

- *Absent Nightmare Zinnias: Rhymed Acrostics from A to Z*

- *What's in Santa's Sleigh This Christmas?*

Readers are invited to follow Linda Ann Nickerson on Twitter (LindaAnnNickers) or Google+ (Linda Ann Nickerson) or to join the Nickers and Ink Facebook page.

Stealing Wonder

A Rhyming Race to Capture Grace

www.ingramcontent.com/pod-product-compliance
Lightning Source LLC
Chambersburg PA
CBHW062008040426
42447CB00010B/1970